Wake Up America!

A compilation of the greatest conspiracies by the ComSocs to destroy our country.

Rescue our diminishing future by facing reality before it is too late.

Norman Hall

Kristy St Pere

Disclaimer

All contents here-in are believed to be factual and convincing. Therefore, W. Norman Hall and Kristina St. Pere, Authors, shall be held harmless of interpretations, inaccuracies, misquoting or omissions from liability.

Table of Contents

This book is dedicated

to my departed wife

Sylvia

Loving and Protective of family

A true Patriot

Loved our country

An Avid Reader of Books

Quote from President Ronald Reagan

During an interview, he was asked
about his earlier years as a Democrat.

He stated, "The Party Left Me."

Acknowledgements

The data that is stored on the website is fantastic. However, the most vital and disturbing news from the website were acquired by the research efforts of my daughter, Kristina. We often discuss political issues. Kristy is like her mother. She can fire back a political opinion in a split second. Likewise with my son, Chris. We often discuss politics too. He is definitely a "chip off the old block". Both love their country. Both are true patriots. Yes, I am a proud father.

Thanks to the Richmond Times-Dispatch for their pro and con articles, and the editors, and the authors of commentaries who write with concern and love of their country – the United States of America.

On a scale of 1 to 10, the Richmond Times Dispatch rates a 10!

Thanks to the editors of listed magazines.

The titles of articles and the author's names are listed under the heading news commentaries and contents.

Special sincere thanks to Baron Bodissy and Martin Mawyer – the true USA patriots – for all their efforts to inform all of the USA citizens of the dangers of radical Muslims in the USA.

Special sincere thanks to Michael Thomas for his exhaustive investigation website document of Barack Obama's forged birth certificate.

Great thanks to the author of *AccidentalPatroit.blog* at *Wordpress.com/TheFlounderTheme*

Thanks for the website document "100 Percent Fed-Up" by Michele Malkin. It is an excellent Wake-Up document. Anyone who cares about our educational system must contact Michele Malkin on the website. Michele is a very intelligent lady. Thank you, thank you patriot Michele.

From the Authors

An important lesson that was learned from being complacent – I am not bragging, but I believe this is a good illustration:

On the high school track team, I won the district high jump trophy. I was a strong contender in the low hurdles. I was ahead, nearing the finish line, thinking I would win. I slacked my momentum, my school friend shot by me and won by approximately 1 foot at the finish line.

The lesson I learned and have never forgotten – never slacken near the finish line whatever your endeavor may be in an honest direction.

Always try to put a little extra effort in your duties. The trophies are there to win.

The inaction of our elected officials in Congress to seriously confront the dangers to our political system is a danger to all of us.

The inaction, the complacency, the lack of the citizenry to wake-up, inform themselves of reality prompted us to accumulate past and present news commentaries. Please – realize the truth and take action to protect our constitution.

Norman Hall

My dad and I, my brother Chris, and our families have great concerns for the future of the United States. Therefore, we are trying to do our patriotic duty by taking action to inform the citizenry of the truth,

Kristy St. Pere

Health and Faith

Take time TO LAUGH
>It is the music of the soul.

Take time TO THINK
>It is the source of power.

Take time TO PLAY
>It is the source of perpetual youth.

Take time TO READ
>It is the fountain of wisdom.

Take time TO PRAY
>It is the greatest power on earth.

Take time TO LOVE AND BE LOVED
>It is a God-given privilege.

Take time TO BE FRIENDLY
>It is the road to happiness

Take time TO GIVE
>It is too short a day to be selfish

Take time To Work
>It is the price of success.

Take time TO ENJOY GOOD FOOD
>It is the source of health.

Take Time
Author Unknown

Please Activate
The Thinking Process

The information contained in this book is from the news media reporting the news of the 1900s through 2014. For verification, the reader should research the media archives and websites.

1. We have been and we are still being brainwashed – Wake Up United States of America!

2. Our freedom is being used to destroy our freedom.

3. **Wake Up Voters!** Voters must force the United States Congress to pass a law limiting our elected officials to two (2) four-year terms maximum.

Retelling History for the Uninformed and the Young

For our elected officials and for the freebie takers: The United States has acquired the status of not being the richest nation on the planet earth.

The United States has lost some academic status to countries that may surprise you.

The following contents should be read with an open mind and an understanding what the election of the President and some members of Congress in 2016 will bequeath to the future of the United States.

WARNING

COMPLACENCY

IS NOT AN OPTION

Chapter 1
Introduction

My Concern

Over the years, I have collected news articles, watched the television news, and listened to the radio. In addition, I have had conversations with a former member of Governor Jimmy Carter's administration. I was convinced President Jimmy Carter was indoctrinating socialism as President of the United States.

Likewise, I was convinced President Bill Clinton was indoctrinating Socialism in the United States.

Carter and Clinton were successful it seems, unnoticed in doing their part in advancing the planned agenda.

President Barack Obama capitalized on the previous successful agenda, and his training as a convincing speaker enabled him to be successful in advancing socialism's movement. He has powerful secret support. Did Jimmy Carter and Bill Clinton have the same secret group support as Barrack Obama?

The dumbing down of our educational structure, unwillingness of many citizens who do not seek the truth, the complacency of thinking their lives will not be harmed - a great concern. (See Chapter 2)

The compliancy ones should read the books titled <u>Pinheads and Patriots</u> by Bill O'Reilly and <u>Glenn Beck's Common Sense</u> by Glenn Beck.

A Ten Fold Concern

1. The Chinese President "sees Asian-led world order." He said the gunboat diplomacy of the United States is a threat to peace.

2. In addition to the dangers of the ComSocs (Chapter 2), we have a Muslim radical organization well established in the United States. I believe their goal is to destroy all humans who do not believe in their form of religion. Their women are used as baby factories to increase their population.

3. The average citizen does not have a clue as to the undercurrent conspiracy that is in full force; the lies; the brainwashing; using federal agencies to reduce the liberties of the United States citizens to ultimately take over as a one-government rule.

4. In the 1960's, our citizens were subjected to brainwashing as young adults. It seems to be the reason some children are allowed to spend too many hours on technology gadgets, not realizing the brainwashing harm they are receiving at present.

5. All citizens must wake up to reality and to the real truth. Too many citizens think the federal government is a huge bank that will be giving them freebies the rest of their lives. The young male at a California beach was not concerned about the nation's problems; he was having fun collecting his USA freebie check.

6. No elected official should be allowed to remain in congress for 34 – 40 years. Two four-year terms must be the maximum. In appealing to the good judgment of the citizenry of the United States, all must seek the truth from our elected officials and hold them accountable.

7. Please study and take seriously the ramifications of a ComSoc one-rule government that is brainwashing our citizenry. Do we as citizens want more of the same of the Obama Administration?

8. The ComSocs are on the race bandwagon to further divide the United States (see Chapter 2).

9. For the uninformed, the definitions of the words below from the Merriam-Webster Dictionary are not the true definition in the political structure of the United States. The word *liberal* and the word *democrat* are misleading to many citizens of the United States, unfortunately, and more so for the immigrants to the United States who vote Democratic.

10. The word liberal in the United States is Socialism. The word *Democrat, Democratic Party* and the word *Left* are all defined as *Socialism*. <u>The Democratic Party was stolen years ago.</u> Their actions have convinced me to state the above opinion. My appeal to the true Democrat – Take your party back and do not be brainwashed in a crossover-voting scheme.

Chapter 2
Greatest Conspiracies

Complacency May Be Your Adversity

Brain Washing Speeches – We are Told the Big Lie

Any elected official who does not have the ability to help or solve the nation's problems in four (4) or eight (8) years (a long time) should not be allowed to remain in the United States Congress. Term limits of eight (8) years would solve approximately 50% of our nation's problems.

Our freedom and our way of life during the 1940's and 1950's has changed dramatically over the years to the present time. For those who did not live in the earlier years and therefore did not experience that way of life do not have the knowledge to compare the life and teaching of 2014 with the truth of the earlier years. We strongly urge readers to encourage the non-readers to read the following contents.

Wake Up United States of America

In the 1900's, the Marxists infiltrated local groups to help in organizing protest marches concerning labor and the political structure. In later years, the Marxists were called communists. They made great efforts to infiltrate the Unites States Congress. Later they determined their efforts would make more progress by infiltrating local and national organizations, our learning establishments and political institutions.

Greatest Conspiracies

The Communists were not shy about their intentions. There were numerous news articles about Communism in the media when President Ronald Reagan put the pressure on the Communist Soviet Union (Russia). Under Reagan, the CIA sabotaged the soviets.

A news reporter interviewed the Chairman of the Communist Party of the United States. The reporter asked Gus Hall what the plans of the USA Communist Party were, now that the Soviet Union has collapsed. Gus Hall stated the party would go underground, meaning the Communists would infiltrate quietly. Gus Hall died on October 13, 2000 at the age of 90. The new chair is Sam Webb.

During President Ronald Reagan's term, he called a Communist a Communist and a Socialist a Socialist. During a speech on television, he stated "I have had it up to my keister".

The words Communist and Socialist were rarely mentioned after Ronald Reagan's term as President. Political correctness became the proper method. A communist and a socialist were now called by new names: Left and Liberal. The brainwashing had succeeded.

The Communists have infiltrated all of society where a lot of people have become socialist and communist, some not realizing or understanding reality. When a reporter interviewed a person from Hollywood, California on the television program USA Presidents, he stated he was a Communist. Even the Ford Foundation was infiltrated. The communists infiltrated the Nobel Peace Prize organization. From the news media – finally, an award to Malala Yousafzai. Good move.

To advance the accusation "Let's Call It Like It Is", I believe we should combine the Communist and Socialist Parties into one party and call them the "ComSoc Party".

Sadly, many good and decent people who vote Democratic and Republican do not understand that the Democratic Party was stolen

<u>years ago</u>. Again, they have been brainwashed. True Democrats – take your party back!

The main goal of the ComSoc Party is to destroy the moral unity base of families. How many people recall that, in the 1960's, the ComSocs trying to brainwash the young by telling them not to trust anyone over 30 years of age. This included their parents. Brainwashing and dumbing-down the young had begun.

The ComSocs other vital goals were to destroy the educational base, disrupt our moral structure, destroy our industrial system, and our monetary system. As Nikita Khrushchev, past leader of Communist Russia, stated it was their goal to divide and conquer the United States from within; to divide the races – black against white; to destroy the USA as a world military power; to reduce the USA to a third world nation under one government rule. This is happening to the United States with Barrack Obama as President. <u>The Communist Party Convention was in June 13-15, 2014 in Chicago, Illinois.</u>

<u>Conclusion</u>

The ComSoc Party is very patient. All of the misery the United States of America is experiencing as of 2014 is through the successful efforts of the ComSoc Party with Barack Obama helping knowingly or unknowingly.

For those who do not understand how the ComSocs are successful, just try some deep thinking after reading the following example. Each ComSoc will do their part to accomplish the goal regardless of the time it takes.

Please read the following chart:

> - Take a piece of wood ½" x ½" x 3" and secure it
> - Take a sharp knife and cut a chip from the piece of wood.
> - Then cut another chip.
> - Keep chipping away until all of the wood is down to the last chip.
> - This illustrates how our freedom and rights – our Constitution – is being destroyed.
> **Wake Up America!**

From the Merriam-Webster Dictionary:

com·mu·nism

noun \ˈkäm-yə-ˌni-zəm, -yü-\

A way of organizing a society in which the government owns the things that are used to make and transport products (such as land, oil, factories, ships, etc.) and there is no privately owned property

a : a theory advocating elimination of private property

b : a system in which goods are owned in common and are available to all as needed

2 *capitalized*
a : a doctrine based on revolutionary Marxian socialism and Marxism-Leninism that was the official ideology of the Union of Soviet Socialist Republics

b : a totalitarian system of government in which a single authoritarian party controls state-owned means of production

c : a final stage of society in Marxist theory in which the state has withered away and economic goods are distributed

so·cial·ism

anoun \ˈsō-shə-ˌli-zəm\

A way of organizing a society in which major industries are owned and controlled by the government rather than by individual people and companies

1: any of various economic and political theories advocating collective or governmental ownership and administration of the means of production and distribution of goods
2*a* : a system of society or group living in which there is no private property
b : a system or condition of society in which the means of production are owned and controlled by the state
3: a stage of society in Marxist theory transitional between capitalism and communism and distinguished by unequal distribution of goods and pay according to work done

Chapter 3
100 Percent FED Up

Parents and non-parents who care about the progressive indoctrination of our youth and public and private schools – this is an important read about the <u>Common Core</u> curriculum which will be controlled by the federal government

<u>Rotten to the Core: Obama's War on Academic Standards (Part 1)By Michelle Malkin • January 23, 2013 09:43 AM</u>

(Reprinted with permission)

This year, I'll be using my syndicated column and blog space to expose how progressive "reformers" — mal-formers — are corrupting our schools. One of my New Year's resolutions is to provide you in-depth coverage of this vital issue that too often gets shunted off the daily political/partisan agenda. While the GOP tries to solve its ills with better software and communications consultants, the conservative movement — and America — face much larger problems. It doesn't start with the "low-information voter." <u>It starts with the no-knowledge student.</u> This is the first in an ongoing series on "Common Core," the stealthy federal takeover of school curriculum and standards across the country. As longtime readers know, my own experience with this ongoing sabotage of academic excellence dates back to my early reporting on the Clinton-era "Goals 2000" and "outcome-based" education and extends to my recent parental experience with "Everyday Math".

The good news is that grass-roots education and parental groups, brave teachers, and professors are fighting back. See the resource list/links at the bottom of this column and stay tuned for much more.

***

A Must Watch video:

http://www.youtube.com/watch?v+coRNJluF204&feature=player_e mbedded

by Michelle Malkin

America's downfall doesn't begin with the "low-information voter." It starts with the no-knowledge student.

For decades, collectivist agitators in our schools have chipped away at academic excellence in the name of fairness, diversity and social justice. "Progressive" reformers denounced Western civilization requirements, the Founding Fathers and the Great Books as racist. They attacked traditional grammar classes as irrelevant in modern life. They deemed ability grouping of students (tracking) bad for self-esteem. They replaced time-tested rote techniques and standard algorithms with fuzzy math, inventive spelling and multicultural claptrap.

Under President Obama, these top-down mal-formers — empowered by Washington education bureaucrats and backed by misguided liberal philanthropists led by billionaire Bill Gates — are now presiding over a radical makeover of your children's school curriculum. It's being done in the name of federal "for" standards that do anything but raise achievement standards.

Common Core was enabled by Obama's federal stimulus law and his Department of Education's "Race to the Top" gimmickry. The administration bribed cash-starved states into adopting unseen instructional standards as a condition of winning billions of dollars in grants. Even states that lost their bids for Race to the Top money were required to commit to a dumbed-down and amorphous curricular "alignment."

In practice, Common Core's dubious "college- and career"-ready standards undermine local control of education, usurp state autonomy over curricular materials, and foist untested, mediocre and incoherent pedagogical theories on America's schoolchildren.

The information listed above are a few excerpts from Michele Malkins website document which, in my opinion, tells the true story of educational conspiracy. The citizenry of the United States must make the effort to educate themselves about what is transpiring politically for their own well-being. Do not assume anything in today's politics. We urge you sincerely to contact Michele Malkin on her website. If you do not have access to the internet, go to your library for help.

Michele's website address is:

http://michelemalkin.com/2013/23/rotten-to-the-core-obamas-war-on-academic-standards-part-1/

<u>*Notice: The listing below is a vital lesson for parents*</u>

If a child lives with criticism, he learns to condemn . . .
If a child lives with hostility, he learns to fight . . .
If a child lives with fear, he learns to be apprehensive . . .
If a child lives with pity, he learns to feel sorry for himself . . .
If a child lives with ridicule, he learns to be shy . . .
If a child lives with jealousy, he learns to feel envy . . .
If a child lives with shame, he learns to feel guilty ...

BUT
If a child lives with tolerance, he learns to be patient . . .
If a child lives with encouragement, he learns to be confident . . .
If a child lives with praise, he learns to be appreciative . . .
If a child lives with acceptance, he learns to love . .
If children live with approval, they learn to like themselves..
If a child lives with honesty, he learns what truth is . . .

Norman Hall and Kristy St Pere

If a child lives with fairness, he learns justice . . .
If children live with recognition, they learn to have a goal.
If children live with sharing, they learn to be generous.
If a child lives with security, he learns to have faith in himself and
those about him . . .
If a child lives with friendliness, he learns the world is a nice place in
which to live . . ."

Dorothy Law Nolte

One of the most beautiful sounds to my ears is the laughter of small children. Our children - our future.

Norman Hall

Warning

News Announcement

September 14, 2014 – Approximately 7:30 AM on CBS television a lady being interviewed announced the formation of a program, "Barrack Obama and the <u>ACLU</u> to teach kids the constitution". Is this another brainwashing scheme by Obama to distort the real meaning of our constitution in the minds of our young children from grade school through college? (Your opinion of what will happen.) Parents and all citizens of the USA not only must, you are compelled to save our children's minds and our country, the USA.

Chapter 4
Complacency May Be Your Adversity

Wake up United States of America - The Conspiracy has Gained Momentum

News Commentaries – Articles the average citizen never reads

The following are titles of media articles that tell the story of what is happening to the United States of America over the years of complacency. We must reclaim our country! The articles listed are by reporters who have deep concerns for the future of America. The diminishing of the United States was and still is caused by citizens complacency and voting habits. Remember: you reap what you sow.

(NOTE: Please do not confuse the acronym ACLU with ACLJ. They are different law firms.)

The following listing 1 to 10 were collected up to December 2007:

1. In the 1960's and 1970's, a reported from Richmond Times Dispatch was concerned that the actions of the ACLU were involved in an adverse direction.

2. The ACLU and their followers had a lawsuit in Florida to ban the word "Bible" from a library – Richmond Times Dispatch

3. The United States Congress granted the ACLU $50,000 dollars in a lawsuit to sue the federal judicial system in a civil case. (From the Richmond Times Dispatch) (This is a good

example of what our elected clowns in Congress are doing with our tax dollars.) WNH

4. During December of 2005, the mayor of Denver, Colorado told churches they could not put nativity scenes on the grounds of church properties. Reverend George Morrison of Faith Bible Church rallied his congregation and other church groups to force the mayor to back down. – Richmond Times Dispatch

5. A church group in North Carolina was notified not to place a nativity scene on church property. Pastor Wooden rallied his congregation to fight the ACLU. Another church congregation received a "no nativity scene notice". The church congregation raised $9,000 dollars to fight the ACLU – The Richmond Times Dispatch

6. In another case, a library was planning to install a nativity scene on library property. The ACLU notified the library officials to refrain from putting symbols of baby Jesus or the cradle, or any other figures representing human beings. They were given permission to only display a straw hut with symbols of animals – Richmond Times Dispatch.

7. The multi-millionaire who was funding Howard Dean in his run for president was giving large sums of money to the ACLU. – Richmond Times Dispatch

8. The Discovery Methodist Church in Richmond, Virginia chose to put a simulated nativity scene on church property. A pole-framed shelter with plastic covering was erected to shelter live animals standing in the cold weather. There were no symbols of baby Jesus, a cradle, or human like figures. – Richmond Times Dispatch

9. No church denominational headquarters and only a few church congregations have rallied to get on the backs of a questionable United States Congress to act against the ACLU.

10. Around 1972, The National Council of Churches met in Boston to have a conference on nuclear electric power and

nuclear bombs. When the church groups from across the nation met, a reporter at the conference discovered there were 12 Communist infiltrators who were able to gain control of the conference and instigated protest marches.– Richmond Times Dispatch

11. Whatever Happens, It's Someone Else's Fault by Paul Greenburg

12. Media Academic Elite Mislead America with Myths by Walter Williams

13. Mr. President: I Did Build My Business by Ben Bruno

14. Citizens Willingly Relinquish Liberty by Walter Williams

15. In Some Ways We Are A Nation Of Cowards (stated by Eric Holder, Attorney General of the United States) by Walter Williams (Eric Holder is the coward making such a statement, surrounded by secret service agents – WNH)

16. In 1999, the Christian Coalition director Randy Tate stated, "It makes it tough to teach kids right from wrong in the sense that the president doesn't know right from wrong." – The Associated Press

17. Folks Have Lost The Freedom To Say What They Think – Walter Williams

18. Want To Glimpse The Future? Read On by John W Martin and Gary L Rhodes

19. No Room For Complacency – European Commission Downgrades Forecasts – The Associated Press

20. Citizens Must Endorse Vision Of The Future by Rachel Flynn

21. Common Sense In Short Supply by Ann Landers

22. Use Of The Word Lady Is Found To Be Offensive To One Reader, by Miss Manners (The way I understood the article, this person said using the word "lady" was sexist and it made

her cringe. What planet is she from? The words "lady" and "gentlemen" are the highest of honors – by WNH)

23. The increasing number of socialists is alarming. Now they want the word "master" removed from "master bedroom".

24. Jimmy Carter Still Criticizing The United States – from Birmingham, England and Atlanta, Georgia

25. Americans Give Scant Allegiance To The United States Constitution - by Walter Williams

26. <u>Why Do Successful Societies Seem To Give Up</u> - by Victor Davis Hanson

27. <u>Who Cares About Our Future</u> - by Walter Williams

28. <u>Treason To The Constitution </u> - by Gary McDowell

29. Wilder's Advice – Incendiary – The Former Virginia Governor Douglas Wilder Urges Obama To Change His Staff

30. Despite Campaign Promises, Obama's Not Telling The Truth - by Robert Samuelson

31. <u>Oppression: Recall Socialism's Communism's Horrors</u> – by Walter Williams

32. <u>Why Does SSA Need All That Ammunition</u>? – The Associated Press

33. Success Story – I Am Black – Not African American – Stated By James Brown, A Well Know Singer And Entertainer – by The Associated Press

34. <u>Bogus – What Is and Isn't A Right</u>? – by Walter Williams

35. Slave Ownership Was Begun In Virginia By An African – by Edward J. Toner, Jr of Brick, New Jersey

36. <u>History – Slavery Was Much More Than A Southern Problem</u> – by L. Douglas Wilder, former black governor of Virginia

37. Where Have All The Flower Children Gone? – by The Associated Press

38. Respect For The Constitution - by Walter Williams

39. Legislation – Bill Puts ACLU Cash Cow In The Cross Hairs; Support Of HR 2679. The Public Expression Of Religion Act Of 2005 The Bill's Aims Were To End ACLU's Abuse Of A 1976 Law. The ACLU Collects Millions In Tax Payer Dollars – by The American Legion Magazine

40. Supreme Court Sent The Game Into Extra Innings – by editor, Richmond Times Dispatch. The editor's comments abridged as follows: Chief Justice John Roberts has often employed a baseball analogy. The Affordable Care Act. He threw a huge curveball by legislating from the bench. He may have committed a Constitutional error in that Article 1, Section 1 of the Constitution clearly states "…all bills for raising revenue shall originate in the house".

41. Public Opinion – Ruling? What Ruling? – Editorial page, Richmond Times Dispatch. According to the Pew Research Center, 45 percent of Americans either did not know that the high court had upheld the Affordable Care Act, or thought it had struck down the law – further proof that the American Proletariat is a bunch of slack-jawed ignoramuses.

42. Acknowledge Militant Islam's Threat, Then We Can Counter It – by Elizabeth Larus

43. Kill 'Em All…We Have A Strategy Drawn Up For The Destruction Of Anglo-Saxon Civilization – by Hassan Abbasi, the Iranian strategist

44. Michigan Bill Would Block Use Of Islamic Law. A Muslin Rights Group Wants The Islamic Law To Be Part Of The Constitutional Right Law – by The Associated Press

45. "World War III To Start Approximately 1994-1999 With The Bombing Of New York City. First Trade Center Activity To

Last 20 Years. Then Stated The War Would End In The Year 3797 – predictions by Nostradamus"

46. Many conspiracies have penetrated our society (refer to Chapter 2). Our country is being destroyed from within. We must stop thinking everything will be okay and we can always reverse the politics of the country. Guess what! As of 2014, we must begin to change Obama's change and change back to our Constitution. Election 2016 must not allow an illegal president.

47. In Virginia in 2012 there were 950,000 foreign born residents. Most were of Hispanic origin, the ninth largest immigrant population in the United States.

48. *We Are All Becoming Ignorant* – by Carlyle P. Comer in a letter to the editor of Richmond times Dispatch

49. Try to understand this "Mind Twister" – from Richmond Times Dispatch – not old news. Washington, DC – The Socialist Workers Party has <u>been allowed to keep its donors secret with special protection by the Federal Election Commission</u>. Guess What! The Socialist Workers Party advocates a Marxist Revolution to overthrow the United States Government. How stupid is this! Again, throw the bums out of congress with Barack Obama.

50. <u>Law Bars Release Of Obama Birth Information, Honolulu</u> – from Richmond Times Dispatch

51. <u>Washington – Federal Workers Owe $3.5 Billion Dollars In Back Taxes As Of September 30, 2011</u> – from Richmond Times Dispatch. Barack Obama elected President in 2008.

52. Atlanta, Georgia – Human rights violations by the United States during War on Terrorism could allow dictators to justify their own abuses – <u>stated the brilliant past President Jimmy Carter, always criticizing the United States</u> – from Richmond Times Dispatch. (Underlined comments by W N Hall)

53. Birmingham, England – Jimmy Carter said in a news conference that the detention of terror suspects at the Guantanamo Bay Naval Base was an embarrassment, an excuse to attack the United States, and a disgrace to the USA. (Jimmy Carter – you were one of the worst Presidents of the USA. If you dislike the USA leave it. I will help with a one-way ticket – article from Richmond Times Dispatch. Underlined comments by W N Hall.

54. Quote of the day: Former Senator Orrin Hatch said (referring to the Clinton Administration): We also have to acknowledge the bold, steady instinctive use of all the modern means of communication to dissemble, mislead, and fool the people as well as to cover up official corruption – excerpt from article by Richmond Times Dispatch

55. Lexington, Virginia – Former President Jimmy Carter's remarks (after receiving a Virginia Military Institute's *Johnathan M Daniels Humanitarian Award for Public Service:* Still criticizing the Unites States, saying the United States Electoral system is flawed and unfair to underprivileged voters. Where did Carter get his hogwash, sociological brainwashing training? Was it at the place as that of Bill Clinton and Barack Obama? The ComSoc's agenda is to destroy our electoral systems. Do not believe what Jimmy Carter preaches about all the laws and our constitution are unfair and flawed. If our electoral system is flawed, maybe that is how Jimmy Carter was elected President of the United States.

Our voting system – some data is as follows: The President of the United States is not elected by the popular vote.

A few years ago an article in the newspaper stated, if I recall correctly, five large cities with large populations could elect a president. Therefore, our founders were very intelligent with good future insights that led to drafting an electoral college. For example: The State of Virginia has thirteen electoral votes. Each of two senators and each of eleven representatives has one electoral vote. The state authority adds the electoral votes to the proper affiliated party. The total electoral votes for the USA are 538. The candidate must receive 270 electoral votes to win the election for the President of the United States. The population of each state dictates the number of electoral votes. To be verified. Also from website

56. An article from the *Parade Magazine, 2002* – Our survey says nearly 90% blame a lack of parental involvement as the leading cause of school violence.

57. Remembering Malaise – Carter's Foreign Policy Cancelled Itself Out – by Paul Greenberg, 2002, Richmond Times Dispatch

58. Mandela Slams US, Britain On Iraq – by Associated Press, Richmond Times Dispatch

59. *Obama Has Eroded Our Work Ethic* – letter to the editor by Martin Shorter, Richmond Times Dispatch

60. 2008 – Only 18 Shun Pork Projects – Rest Of Lawmakers Eagerly Snapped Up $18 Billion Worth – by the Associated Press, Richmond Times Dispatch

61. White House: No Price for Obama Access: excerpts from article revealing a new group called *Organizing for Action*, supporting President Barack Obama's agenda. The news media asked White House spokesperson Jay Carney about reports that $500,000 will give access to quarterly meetings with Obama.

62. 2014 – Study: Fuels from corn waste aren't better than gas – excerpt from article – Biofuels made from the leftovers of harvested corn plants are worse than gasoline for global warming in the short term, a study shows, challenging the Obama Administration's conclusions that they are a much cleaner oil alternative and will help combat climate change. Corn Biofuel Release 7% More Greenhouse Gases Compared With Gasoline – by The Associated Press in Richmond Times Dispatch

63. Holder: Restore Felon's Rights: the Attorney General says millions are disenfranchised by their inability to vote. (Eric Holder is doing his part of the agenda to assure millions of votes for the ComSoc party (refer to Chapter 2) under the name of the Democrat Party. It is very clear what the scheme indicates – with the hope of the black vote, the approximate 12 million illegal votes and the legal Latinos vote together with other foreign-born citizens, the Obama group will win the 2016 election. If this scheme becomes true, the life in the United States will be altered dramatically to a one-rule government. Wake-Up America. This is the reason for this book. From News Media.

64. We're Surrendering Our Civil Liberties – a must-read article written by Leonard Pitts and available on the internet at LPITS@miamiherald.com with media service – taken from Richmond Times Dispatch.

65. 2012 – Obama Plans Major Push On Immigration – McClatchy Newspapers from Richmond Times Dispatch

66. May 27, 2013- Kerry Backs $4 Billion Plan For West Bank – The Washington Post, by Anne Gearan and William Booth. [A stupid move by the Obama Administration (money will be passed on to the terrorists in my opinion) The USA is in debt in the trillions of dollars – owing trillions of dollars of debt to China. The taxpayers are forced to pay.]

67. Another great problem: Census Says New Gauge Shown High Of 49.7 Million Poor In United States – by Associated Press, from Richmond Times Dispatch.

68. Affordable Care Act: Mr. President You Lied – by Leonard Pitts, from Richmond Times Dispatch

69. (Our judicial system is in danger) Editorial article titled 4th Circuit Drifting Left

Excerpt from the article: Appointments – one by Bill Clinton (Robert Bruce King); two by Barack Obama (Andre Davis and Albert Diaz). Obama has now appointed six of the jurists on the court. Democrats now have a 3-2 ratio – from The Richmond Times Dispatch. With this type of ratio across the United States, not knowing how many are liberals, lefts, or whatever name a person chooses, the USA is in deep trouble.

70. *Constitution in the Crosshairs* – Letter to the Editor, The Richmond Times Dispatch by Katherine Noble

71. *Technology – Internet Armageddon* - Has the Federal Government and industry solved the mystery as to how China's army could penetrate the infrastructure of the United States? From the News Media.

72. California: During a demonstration, a Latino in a loud voice – We are going to take California back. The News Media

73. All immigrants must learn English before becoming USA citizens, for their own economic welfare and less of a burden on the USA economic system. (WNH)

"Notice" Interesting Data 2013-2014

2013 – from USA Quick Facts, the USA Census Bureau

Population 2010 (April 1)...........................308,747,716
Population 2013, Increased........................316,128,839
Radio News Commentary 2014
(Immigration crossed borders) Approximately... 10,000,000
(To be verified - up to 2014)

Black Alone..	13.2%
American Indian and Native Alaska.........	1.2%
Asian Alone.......................................	5.3%
Islanders Alone..................................	0.2%
Other Races, Middle East, Etc. 2013............	2.4%
Hispanic or Latino – 2013........................	17.7%
White Alone...	62.6%

Percentage adds to slightly over 100%

Chapter 5
Communist Goals (1963)

Congressional Record – Appendix, pp. A34-A35

January 10, 1963

Current Communist Goals

Extension of Remarks of Hon. A. S. Herlong, Jr. of Florida

In the House of Representatives

Thursday, January 10, 1963

Mr. HERLONG. Mr. Speaker, Mrs. Patricia Nordman of De Land, Fla., is an ardent and articulate opponent of communism, and until recently published the De Land Courier, which she dedicated to the purpose of alerting the public to the dangers of communism in America.

At Mrs. Nordman's request, I include in the RECORD, under unanimous consent, the following "Current Communist Goals," which she identifies as an excerpt from "The Naked Communist," by Cleon Skousen:

[From "The Naked Communist," by Cleon Skousen]

Not knowing who or if anyone in the United States Congress had a real concern about Communism, other than our past patriot,

President Ronald Reagan, I found the speech by Hon. A.S. Herlong as documented was electrifying.

When I received the website document "Communist Goals (1963)" on March 22, 2013 it pleased me greatly in giving my years of rhetoric some credibility. I do not know of any other document that tells the truth with great concern for the United States as of 2014.

Every citizen of the United States must read or be told about this document. Communism is still operating strongly in the United States. The data should be a shocking reality for the uninformed.

All citizens should wake up out of complacency and apply pressure on our "do nothing Congress" when in session.

Contact Forest Glen Durland at

www.uhuh.com or log on to the website:

www.uhuh.com/nwo/communism/comgoals.htm

Expert Brainwashing

From the website "Expert Brainwashing, Refer to Chapter 2

All the reiterate and accusations, distortions, untruths the Communists-Socialists keep inflicting on the citizens, the citizens of color, they stated, in their continuous effort to divide the races – black against white. Their efforts are focused on distorting and destroying the industrial base and our constitution. These ComSocs live in the United States with all of the protection afforded by the Constitution as citizens.

My Advice? Anyone not liking the USA – Leave it (WNH).

Announcing the Communist Party Convention,

June 2014!

by: Communist Party USA
November 27 2013
tags: CPUSA, Party Convention, 95 years

Put people before profits: Help build a movement to transform this country

[A business must make a profit to maintain employees – otherwise who is going to pay the salaries? WNH]

Announcing the 30th Convention of the Communist Party USA

June 13-15, 2014, Chicago, Illinois

The people of the United States face enormous challenges today. **[Again, ComSoc brainwashing. Yes, because of Barack Obama and ComSocs.] WNH**

We live in a capitalist system where the 99% of people struggle every day to survive and the richest 1% control the vast majority of wealth and power. Capitalism cannot meet the needs of the vast majority. **[Wake Up ComSocs – Face the Truth! Brainwashing and lies. We need paying jobs. WNH]**

Economic inequality and job insecurity are increasing. Working families are living with less and working longer hours. The infrastructure of our cities and towns is deteriorating. Our schools are underfunded and essential public services are strapped and slashed. Home foreclosures are everywhere and millions of people are homeless and hungry **[not true]** *in the richest country in the world. Racism, sexism, homophobia and all kinds of discrimination are commonplace. Working men and women fight and die in wars around the globe for U.S. corporate interests.* **[All above created by ComSocs.]** *WNH*

We also face an urgent threat to the very survival of life on the planet. Climate change is the byproduct of capitalism. **[Not True]** *It is working people, the poor and communities of color who face the most direct consequences of global warming and the poisoning of our environment.* **[Hogwash! WNH]**

The drive of the rich and powerful to gain wealth at the expense of working people is the only logic of capitalism. **[Not True]**

But everywhere in our country people unite to fight to improve their lives, to change the world for the better.

The main obstacle to progress today is right-wing extremism. Right wing spokespeople and groups represent and are funded by the most conservative sections of the rich and powerful.

[Lies. The problems are caused by ComSocs. WNH]

Chapter 6
Close Your Eyes and Think of Sheikh Gilani

March 2, 2013 by Baron Bodissey

An organization known as Jamaat ul-Fuqra ("Community of the Impoverished") was founded about 1980 by a known terrorist, the Pakistani Sufi Sheikh Syed Mubarak Ali Hasmi Shah Gilani. Over several decades JuF has established a network of dozens of rural training compounds across the United States and Canada.

I have written extensively on Jamaat ul-Fuqra in the past. For more on this group and its activities, see the Jamaat ul-Fuqra

Archives. The first post in the series describes my initial visit to Red House in October 2005 — which seems like a million years ago now — and contains a lot of background material on Sheikh Gilani and Jamaat ul-Fuqra.

Mr. Baron Bodisseys unselfish demeanor in listing others who have been inspired by his writings. He listed the most noble and productive among them has been the Christian Action Network in Lynchburg, Virginia. Mr. Bodissey stated Mr. Martin Mawyer, the president of the Christian Action Network, published a book about Jamaat Ul-Fuqua (books were listed).

Above excerpts illustrate a real concern. Log on to his website at:

http://gatesofvienna.net/2013/03/close-your-eyes-and-think-of-sheikh-gilani/

Chapter 7
Jamaat ul-Fuqra in Virginia

October 9, 2005 by Baron Bondissey

During the Beltway Sniper crisis, back in the fall of 2002, a series of articles in The Washington Times described John Allen Muhammad's conversion to Islam, and his later break with the Nation of Islam (the articles are no longer available, but extracts have been preserved at

http://thefiringline.com/forums/archive/index.php/t-140322.html).

Apparently the NOI was not militant enough for Mr. Muhammad, and he left it to become involved with a group called Jamaat ul-Fuqra (Arabic for "community of the impoverished"), a terrorist organization founded by a notorious Pakistani cleric, Sheikh Mubarak Ali Gilani. What drew my eye in the article was the mention of a Jamaat ul-Fuqra compound in Red House, Virginia. Red House?! I know Red House — a small village in rural Charlotte County.

This is a small excerpt from Mr. Baron Bodissey's document. Another vital wake-up call. Obtain this document by logging on to:

http://gatesofvienna.blogspot.com/2005/10/jamaat-ul-fuqra-in-virginia-part-1.html.

This describes a training camp for young Muslim-American men as described by Mr. Bodissey. This is a disturbing website document that I never knew existed. This is probably true for 90%+ of my fellow American citizens as well.

When our elected officials do not sound the alarm regarding this radical Muslim threat and care more about votes from the Muslin citizens in fear of losing an election, or being called a racist, then I say vote those bums out of Congress.

Hopefully we will not forget that a Muslim group in Michigan tried to get legislation passed to add the Muslim Koran to the Constitution of the United States.

Why is the news media keeping the radical Muslim threat quiet?

Chapter 8
An Abomination of Our System

March 9, 2009 by Baron Bodissey

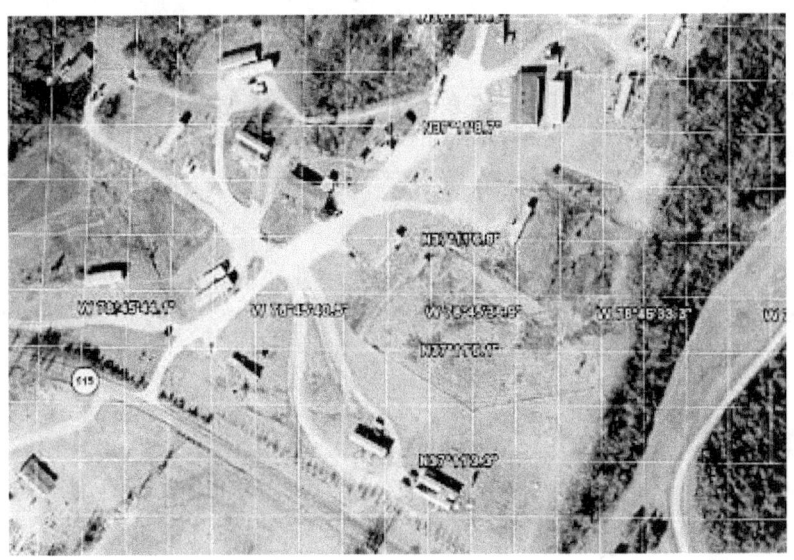

A reader named Roger S., after reading Gates of Vienna, Christian Action Network, The Politics of CP, and other sources that report on Jamaat ul-Fuqra, was inspired to mount a field trip to Red House, Virginia, and do some first-hand investigation of the Muslims of America compound there. He sent us the following report.

Norman Hall and Kristy St Pere

Dear Gates of Vienna,

A fellow concerned Patriot and I were in Charlotte County, Virginia on Thursday doing our a bit of our own surveillance.

The Red House compound and surrounding area were being patrolled and guarded by a couple of black guys dressed as local farm workers in dirty clothes driving a beat up red Ford truck and old grey Chevy truck.

This is an excerpt, which I hope will increase your patriotic spirit. For the complete article, please access his website at:

http://gatesofvienna.blogspot.com/2009/03/abomination-of-our-system.html

Chapter 9
Sheikh Mubarik Gilani

Twilight in America by Martin Mawyer

"They are asleep. They are a bomb. Here is the scariest part ... Anything can happen with MOA at any time."

Those are the words of a young Muslim man named Ali Aziz. Who is he? And what is this dangerous "MOA" that he refers to?

The existence of dozens of Islamic guerrilla warfare training camps located in rural neighborhoods throughout America, and the serious crimes they have already committed—and are planning to commit—should be of concern to all law enforcement officers.

The group known as Muslims of the Americas (MOA), which itself is a front group for a radical terrorist group called Jamaat Al Fuqra (Arabic for "community of the impoverished"), has established dozens of training camps throughout the United States. The group is led by a Muslim cleric in Pakistan, Sheikh Mubarik Gilani.

"They are ready to strike (America) at one word" from Sheikh Gilani, says Ariz.

Gilani preaches to his followers that jihad, holy war, against America was the only path to Islamic purifications. "We are fighting to destroy the enemy" he said. "We are dealing with evil at its roots, and its roots are America."

Martin Mawyer is the Founder and President of Christian Action Network, a non-profit public advocacy and education group based in Lynchburg, Virginia. He began his career as a freelance journalist and has authored several books, including "Silent Shame," "The Pro-Family Contract With America," "Pathways to Success," and his most recent, "Twilight in America: The Untold Story of Islamic Terrorist Training Camps Inside America." He has produced a number of documentary films, including Homegrown Jihad, Islam Rising, Sacrificed Survivors and America's Islamic Threat. Mawyer has appeared on The O'Reilly Factor, Hannity, Larry King Live, Pat Robertson's 700 Club, NBC's Today Show, Entertainment Tonight and Fox and Friends. His latest book, "Twilight in America," co-authored by Patti A. Pierucci, details the activities of Islamic terrorist training camps scattered throughout the United States. It can be purchased atTwilightInAmerica.com, or Amazon.com in book or Kindle version. See more at:

http://www.lawenforcementtoday.com/2012/10/25/twilight-in-america/#sthash.4kUUSzfw.dpuf

These are a few excerpts from Martin Mawyers website <u>An Urgent Wake-Up Call</u>. Obtain the full article at:

http://www.lawenforcementtoday.com/tag/sheikh-mubarik-gilani/

Chapter 10
President Jimmy Carter

When Jimmy Carter was ending his term as Governor of Georgia, he met with a group on a yacht off the coast of Georgia. The purpose of the meeting was to plan his run for the USA presidency.

1. Who were the people at the meeting?

2. Who owned the yacht?

3. Why such an elaborate secret?

Soon after Jimmy Carter was elected, he sent Andrew Young on an overseas trip. When he arrived in Africa, Andrew Young stated in a speech that the United States still had slaves.

1. Why did Jimmy Carter meet with Nelson Mandela in Africa who was the leader of the African National Council (ANC), a Communist organization?

2. Why did Jimmy Carter go to Cuba?

3. Why did Jimmy Carter give away the Panama Canal? (Later a news release stated the Panama Canal was managed by Communist China)

4. Why did Jimmy Carter back the release of Cuban spies held in the United States?

There are many other unanswered questions.

During Jimmy Carter's term, he allowed approximately 150,000 people to immigrate to the United States. It seems they think of the USA as a democracy and vote Democratic with all the freebies. In my opinion, this is what Jimmy Carter was relying on for additional Democratic power. Immigration to be verified.

On the television program The Presidents, a woman who was in the Carter Administration, stated Jimmy Carter and Senator Fulbright chose Bill Clinton to run for President of the United States with Hillary as part of the team.

The true background of Jimmy Carter was never revealed. As President of the United States, he almost destroyed the economy and the military. His lack of leadership was quite revealing.

Jimmy Carter's Greatest Achievements

1. Deploying a rescue team into Iran to liberate United States Service Personnel developed into a disaster.

2. Gave away the Panama Canal. Representative Helen Chenoweth stated the treaty was illegal because Jimmy Carter exceeded his constitutional authority in giving away American property and abrogating an earlier treaty.

3. Jimmy Carter formed the Department of Education, dumbing down our educational system. The following are excerpts from a cartoon by Mr. Brookins, Cartoonist in September 2002 from The Richmond Times Dispatch. Mr. Brookins cartoon contained two images of Jimmy Carter making statements on his knowledge of foreign policy.

   The first Jimmy Carter image caption stated, "In 1977, Iran is an island of stability in one of the most troubled areas of the world.

   The second Jimmy Carter image caption states, "In 2002 Iraq poses no current danger to the United States."

Mr. Brookins, a true Patriot.

Chapter 11
President Bill Clinton

Now it is Bill Clinton's Turn

What was the true background of Bill Clinton and Hillary Rodham Clinton? As the news articles and radio news was busy commenting on the Clintons, a few news items were collected.

1. During Bill Clinton's college years he made a trip to Russia – A radio commentary. True or False?

2. Hillary Rodham, about the same time period, went to Cuba - A radio commentary. True or False?

3. The book Hillary Rodham Clinton wrote, It Takes a Village, was complied with a lot of data she acquired while in Cuba. A radio commentary. True or False?

4. Many of Hillary Rodham Clinton's speeches concerning healthcare carried the message: If you do not acquire health insurance you could be fined, or be fined and go to jail. From a news article – to be verified.

5. Why did Bill Clinton make numerous trips to Africa to visit with Nelson Mandela, ANC leader? Why was he following Jimmy Carter's lead?

6. Why did Madeline Albright go to North Korea during the last of Clinton's term? Why did she make a speech where she stated that the United States should not be the only military power? News Article – True or False?

Nelson Mandela ran for the Office of Prime Minister of South Africa. He won the election. From all the news articles printed at that time, one would think Clinton and Mandela were great friends. According to news articles and the television news, Mandela (at the age of 94) seemed to have a favorable rating and altered thinking.

Bill Clinton, like Jimmy Carter, almost destroyed the military. The difference between the two presidents was Clinton understood a favorable economy that provided easy access to money was mandatory for re-election.

Bill Clinton's Greatest Achievements

1. Aborted the U S Special Forces on two attempts to capture or eliminate Osama Bin Laden.

2. Clinton inherited the give-away canal treaty. Bill Clinton rebuffed members of Congress and military officers' efforts to maintain the Panama Canal.

Chapter 12
Barack Obama

Now it is Barack Obama's Turn

What has our President, Barack Obama achieved from 2008 to 2014? What has he achieved from the promises he outlined in those speeches? The speeches he has made from the beginning of his presidency until today are examples of brainwashing.

Perhaps one of his most noteworthy is the speech he made at the <u>Summit of the Americas</u> opening ceremony in Port of Spain, Trinidad and Tobago. Please read the following speech carefully and take time to list how you interpret his making you feel good – toe tingling speech.

Prepare a scorecard for his years as President of the United States. We have added paragraph numbers to make scoring easier. On your scorecard list all of the paragraph numbers where you agree or disagree with what Mr. Obama has achieved.

The speech begins on the following page.

THE WHITE HOUSE

Office of the Press Secretary

(Port of Spain, Trinidad and Tobago)

For Immediate Release   *April 17, 2009*

REMARKS BY THE PRESIDENT
AT THE SUMMIT OF THE AMERICAS
OPENING CEREMONY
Hyatt Regency
Port of Spain, Trinidad and Tobago
7:30 P.M. EDT

1. Good evening. I am honored to join you here today, and I want to thank Prime Minister Manning, the people of Trinidad and Tobago for their generosity in hosting the Fifth Summit of the Americas. And I want to extend my greetings to all the heads of state, many of who I am meeting for the first time. All of us are extraordinarily excited to have this opportunity to visit this wonderful country -- and as somebody who grew up on an island, I can tell you I feel right at home. (Applause.)

2. It's appropriate and important that we hold this summit in the Caribbean. The energy, the dynamism, the diversity of the Caribbean people inspires us all, and are such an important part of what we share in common as a hemisphere.

3. I think everybody recognizes that we come together at a critical moment for the people of the Americas. Our well-being has been set back by a historic economic crisis. Our safety is endangered by a broad range of threats. But this peril can be eclipsed by the promise of a new prosperity and personal security and the protection of liberty and justice for

all the people of our hemisphere. That's the future that we can build together, but only if we move forward with a new sense of partnership.

4. All of us must now renew the common stake that we have in one another. I know that promises of partnership have gone unfulfilled in the past, and that trust has to be earned over time. While the United States has done much to promote peace and prosperity in the hemisphere, we have at times been disengaged, and at times we sought to dictate our terms. But I pledge to you that we seek an equal partnership. (Applause.) There is no senior partner and junior partner in our relations; there is simply engagement based on mutual respect and common interests and shared values. So I'm here to launch a new chapter of engagement that will be sustained throughout my administration. (Applause.)

5. To move forward, we cannot let ourselves be prisoners of past disagreements. I am very grateful that President Ortega -- (applause) -- I'm grateful that President Ortega did not blame me for things that happened when I was three months old. (Laughter.) Too often, an opportunity to build a fresh partnership of the Americas has been undermined by stale debates. And we've heard all these arguments before, these debates that would have us make a false choice between rigid, state-run economies or unbridled and unregulated capitalism; between blame for right-wing paramilitaries or left-wing insurgents; between sticking to inflexible policies with regard to Cuba or denying the full human rights that are owed to the Cuban people.

6. I didn't come here to debate the past -- I came here to deal with the future. (Applause.) I believe, as some of our previous speakers have stated, that we must learn from history, but we can't be trapped by it. As neighbors, we have a responsibility to each other and to our citizens. And by working together, we can take important steps forward to advance prosperity and security and liberty. That is the 21st century agenda that we come together to enact. That's the new direction that we can pursue.

7. Before we move forward for our shared discussions over this weekend, I'd like to put forward several areas where the United States is committed already to strengthening collective action on behalf of our shared goals.

8. First, we must come together on behalf of our common prosperity. That's what we've already begun to do. Our unprecedented actions to stimulate growth and restart the flow of credit will help create jobs and prosperity within our borders and within yours. We joined with our G20 partners to set aside over a trillion dollars for countries going through difficult times, recognizing that we have to provide assistance to those countries that are most vulnerable. We will work with you to ensure that the Inter-American Development Bank can take the necessary steps to increase its current levels of lending and to carefully study the needs for recapitalization in the future. And we recognize that we have a special responsibility, as one of the world's financial centers, to work with partners around the globe to reform a failed regulatory system -- so that we can prevent the kinds of financial abuses that led to this current crisis from ever happening again, and achieve an economic expansion not just in the United States but all across the hemisphere that is built not on bubbles, but on sustainable economic growth.

9. We're also committed to combating inequality and creating prosperity from the bottom up. This is something that I've spoken about in the United States, and it's something that I believe applies across the region. I've asked Congress for $448 million in immediate assistance for those who have been hit hardest by the crisis beyond our borders. And today, I'm pleased to announce a new Microfinance Growth Fund for the hemisphere that can restart the lending that can power businesses and entrepreneurs in each and every country that's represented here. This is not charity. (Applause.) Let me be clear: This is not charity. Together, we can create a broader foundation of prosperity that builds new markets and powers new growth for all peoples in the hemisphere, because our economies are intertwined.

10. Next, we can strengthen the foundation of our prosperity and our security and our environment through a new partnership on energy. Our hemisphere is blessed with bountiful resources, and we are all endangered by climate change. Now we must come together to find new ways to produce and use energy so that we can create jobs and protect our planet.

11. So today, I'm proposing the creation of a new Energy and Climate Partnership of the Americas that can forge progress to a more secure and sustainable future. It's a partnership that will harness the vision and determination of countries like Mexico and Brazil that have already done outstanding work in this area to promote renewable energy and reduce greenhouse gas emissions. Each country will bring its own unique resources and needs, so we will ensure that each country can maximize its strengths as we promote efficiency and improve our infrastructure, share technologies, support investments in renewable sources of energy. And in doing so, we can create the jobs of the future, lower greenhouse gas emissions, and make this hemisphere a model for cooperation.

12. The dangers of climate change are part of a broad range of threats to our citizens, so the third area <u>where we must work together is to advance our common security</u>.

13. Today, too many people in the Americas live in fear. We must not tolerate violence and insecurity, no matter where it comes from. Children must be safe to play in the street, and families should never face the pain of a kidnapping. Policemen must be more powerful than kingpins, and judges must advance the rule of law. Illegal guns must not flow freely into criminal hands, and illegal drugs must not destroy lives and distort our economy.

14. Yesterday, President Calderón of Mexico and I renewed our commitment to combat the dangers posed by drug cartels. <u>Today, I want to announce a new initiative to invest $30 million to strengthen cooperation on security in the Caribbean</u>. And I have directed key members of my Cabinet to build and sustain relations with their counterparts in the hemisphere to constantly adjust our tactics, to build upon best practices, and

develop new modes of cooperation -- because the United States is a friend of every nation and person who seeks a future of security and dignity.

15. And let me add that I recognize that the problem will not simply be solved by law enforcement if we're not also dealing with our responsibilities in the United States. And that's why we will take aggressive action to reduce our demand for drugs, and to stop the flow of guns and bulk cash south across our borders. (Applause.) And that's why I'm making it a priority to ratify the Illicit Trafficking in Firearms Convention as another tool that we can use to prevent this from happening. And I also am mindful of the statement that's been made earlier, that unless we provide opportunity for an education and for jobs and a career for the young people in the region, then too many will end up being attracted to the drug trade. And so we cannot separate out dealing with the drug issue on the interdiction side and the law enforcement side from the need for critical development in our communities.

16. Finally, we know that true security only comes with liberty and justice. Those are bedrock values of the Inter-American charter. Generations of our people have worked and fought and sacrificed for them. And it is our responsibility to advance them in our time.

17. So together, we have to stand up against any force that separates any of our people from that story of liberty -- whether it's crushing poverty or corrosive corruption; social exclusion or persistent racism or discrimination. Here in this room, and on this dais, we see the diversity of the Americas. Every one of our nations has a right to follow its own path. But we all have a responsibility to see that the people of the Americans [sic] have the ability to pursue their own dreams in democratic societies.

18. There's been several remarks directed at the issue of the relationship between the United States and Cuba, so let me address this. The United States seeks a new beginning with Cuba. I know that there is a longer -- (applause) -- I know there's a longer journey that must be traveled to overcome

decades of mistrust, but there are critical steps we can take toward a new day. I've already changed a Cuba policy that I believe has failed to advance liberty or opportunity for the Cuban people. We will now allow Cuban Americans to visit the islands whenever they choose and provide resources to their families -- the same way that so many people in my country send money back to their families in your countries to pay for everyday needs.

19. Over the past two years, I've indicated, and I repeat today, that I'm prepared to have my administration engage with the Cuban government on a wide range of issues -- from drugs, migration, and economic issues, to human rights, free speech, and democratic reform. Now, let me be clear, I'm not interested in talking just for the sake of talking. But I do believe that we can move U.S.-Cuban relations in a new direction.

20. As has already been noted, and I think my presence here indicates, the United States has changed over time. (Applause.) It has not always been easy, but it has changed. And so I think it's important to remind my fellow leaders that it's not just the United States that has to change. All of us have responsibilities to look towards the future. (Applause.)

21. I think it's important to recognize, given historic suspicions, that the United States' policy should not be interference in other countries, but that also means that we can't blame the United States for every problem that arises in the hemisphere. That's part of the bargain. (Applause.) That's part of the change that has to take place. That's the old way, and we need a new way.

22. The United States will be willing to acknowledge past errors where those errors have been made. We will be partners in helping to alleviate poverty. But the American people have to get some positive reinforcement if they are to be engaged in the efforts to lift other countries out of the poverty that they're experiencing.

23. Every nation has been on its own journey. Here in Trinidad and Tobago, we must respect those differences while celebrating those things that we share in common. Our nations were all colonized by empires and achieved our own liberation. Our people reflect the extraordinary diversity of human beings, and our shared values reflect a common humanity -- the universal desire to leave our children a world that is more prosperous and peaceful than the one that we inherited.

24. So as we gather here, let us remember that our success must be measured by the ability of people to live their dreams. That's a goal that cannot be encompassed with any one policy or communiqué. It's not a matter of abstractions or ideological debates. It's a question of whether or not we are in a concrete way making the lives of our citizens better. It's reflected in the hopes of our children, in the strength of our democratic institutions, and our faith in the future.

25. It will take time. Nothing is going to happen overnight. But I pledge to you that the United States will be there as a friend and a partner, because our futures are inextricably bound to the future of the people of the entire hemisphere. And we are committed to shaping that future through engagement that is strong and sustained, that is meaningful, that is successful, and that is based on mutual respect and equality.

Thank you very much. (Applause.) END   *7:46 P.M. EDT*

Barack Obama's Greatest Achievements

The list is about the length of your arm
There is space to list ten topics

1. He does not always tell the truth

2. He is guiding the USA into a third world nation status

3. He is diminishing our industrial status

4. He is weakening our educational structure

57

5. He is shrinking job opportunities

6. He is diminishing our military strength and status

7. He is recklessly spending taxpayer money; borrowing trillions of dollars from China; giving foreign countries trillions of dollars to boost their economies – yes, believe it or not, millions to China and to the Gaza strip.

8. He is not securing our southern border which has caused an immigration tragedy for the United States

9. He has a secret group which is ruling the United States; he is not the leader

10. He is not punishing the drug cartels. Drugs are destroying our culture.

Some Questions to Ponder:

1. Who knows the mystery of the number 6? Was Obama brought to Hawaii at age 6 months, 6 years or 16 years old.

2. Was he truly born in Hawaii?

3. Why was no response given to a news media article that stated Barack Obama came to the United States in 1979?

4. Where are the articles from the investigating news media reporter who interviewed Obama's brother? Did they interview Obama's uncles, aunts, cousins or other relatives? Where are the follow-up articles on Obama at 16 years of age and his mother when they lived in Indonesia before they came to the United States?

5. Where are the true and unaltered documents stating where Obama was born?

6. Why has the college Obama attended refused to release any data regarding his college record? Why has Obama refused to release it?

7. Obama is brainwashing the American public. A Sociology course listing brainwashing techniques would have Obama earning high marks. Obama is an expert at Sociology. Listen carefully to how he forms a sentence, and then listen very carefully to the words he uses in those sentences. The words that are used are supposed to make you feel at ease; to feel good about the president; to make you feel that he is going to make your life happier and more secure.

8. Barack Obama makes most of his speeches at colleges. Most young people can be brainwashed with less effort. College students are being fed, clothed, and sheltered. Most will only learn when survival depends on themselves.

9. People are being labeled. Those that were called "minorities" are being brainwashed, insulted, degraded and used as pawns in exchange for free money in whatever form. Examples may be found in this document under the title Conclusion.

10. Federal employees are being used as pawns and being promised across the board raises by Obama. This is another brainwashing scheme to bring voters into the ComSoc (Democrat) fold so they will vote in 2016. Their goal is to control Congress. They intend to either amend or ignore the Constitution and make Obama the first ruler of the United States (Chavez style). I believe he is telling our citizens this in his speeches. Listen carefully and see if you interpret them the way I do.

11. Where is there an accounting of all the stimulus money?

12. Where is there an accounting of the sequence results?

13. All of Obamas actions have capitalized on the past successes of Jimmy Carter and Bill Clinton in downgrading the United States. Carter and Clinton almost destroyed the strength of the

military. Now, Obama is doing the same thing by reducing the strength of the military and causing trillions of dollars of debt.

14. Obama is following the strategy of Carter and Clinton with a greater effort on sociology (brainwashing). Obama has proved to the United States citizens that he is an expert at sociology.

15. Where had Obama given a speech to an older audience, other than college students and minority groups?

16. Is Obama a Muslim ComSoc? Is he helping their strategy?

17. Obama is using federal agencies to empower, control, and manage the American people. Obama talks about taxing the rich. Brainwashing again. After all, Obama was in the middle class as a senator; now he is a millionaire.

18. Obama has made it clear he will tax and use all methods available to take money from the rich and distribute it to minorities. How much Obama money was given?

19. Obama keeps spending as much of the borrowed trillions of dollars as he can get his hand on (one trillion equals a thousand billion).

20. Obama's agenda is clear. By the end of his second term, he can reduce the strength and industrial base of the United Stated to a third world status by brainwashing people. He is spending our money and the money of future generations – money that may not be forthcoming. He is doing it to compel people to vote for Democrats in the presidential election of 2016. Blames the Republicans for the USA problems.

21. The ComSoc's are confident they will win the full Congress and the Presidency. They will change the Constitution and turn the political system into a single ruling party (government). The food stamps and welfare checks will disappear. The receivers, hopefully, will wake up. All citizens of the United States must wake up so this does not come to pass.

Greatest Conspiracies

Voters must wake up! The reality is that, as of 2014, the voters have not realized the depth of the trouble being experienced by the United States, or the catastrophe that is ahead if the ComSocs continue to control the government. It is certain that, if they do, we may be heading toward the status of a third world nation, resulting in more conflicts that are international.

During a 2014 television newscast, a guest remarked the people of the United States are dumb. As he continued, I realized he was not degrading their intelligence; he was referring to their lack of good common sense. He went on to say our citizens were uninformed, did not care enough about their country, and were living in their own little worlds.

Shortly thereafter, in another newscast, a television reporter was interviewing people on the streets of a large city, asking various citizens about world events and events within the United States. In the broadcasts, we learned that:

1. Many of the people interviewed had not heard of the attacks on Benghazi in Africa;

2. They did not know the name of the Vice President of the United States;

3. A man in his late 30s or early 40s could not answer questions about the news of the week;

4. A person did not know where the city of Houston was located;

5. One individual said they did not know how to write a check.

Media Follow-Up

One day the media reports on something, and the next day it appears it never happened. For instance, where is the media follow-up and investigation on the following issues?

Why were previous news reports which stated persons of secrecy at a hospital in Hawaii forged Barack Obama's birth certificate simply disappeared? No name was ever revealed as to whom the person was that dated and signed the certificate.

Chapter 13
Obama Birth Certificate

Confirmed Forgery
According to Top Expert

Finally, the Truth was Acquired from the Website

by Michael Thomas
December 15th, 2013
Updated 05/01/2014 at 3:22 pm

No attempt to even hide the forgery by those who fabricated the fraudulent document

The birth certificate in question is actually a purported copy of Barack Obama's original birth certificate which is currently held by Hawaii's Department of Health. This copy was posted in April of 2011 on the official whitehouse.gov website where it still appears today. The following document is an exact copy of what appears on the website.

The excerpt above and the ones that follows, from a document by Michael Thomas reveal a distressing problem for the United States. The lack of action by our elected officials in Congress to uphold the Constitution of the United States has put them in a tenuous position. They are lying and their complacency should be examined.

It is inconceivable that the mainstream media (MSM) has not only avoided this story for over five years; it has gone to extremes to cover up the many "high crimes" involved. Likewise, never in US history has the entire political establishment been AWOL concerning a matter of such national significance and legal import. By neglecting to properly investigate these crimes, the nation is now faced with the prospect of a full-blown constitutional crisis of epic proportions.

YES ... it is that serious and much more!

*Read more: **http://www.storyleak.com/obama-birth-certificate-confirmed-forgery-according-top-experts/#ixzz3CTAieXfh***

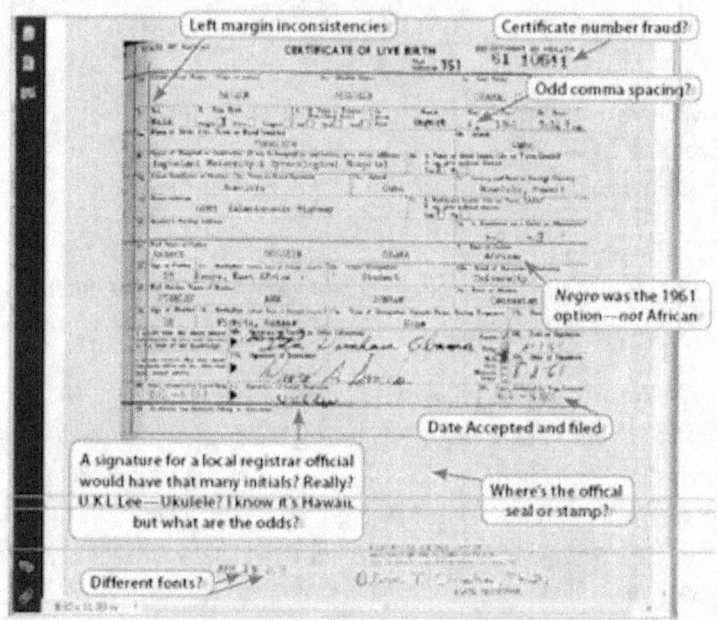

Exhibit 5. Obama birth certificate, 4/27/11. Overall information defies common sense

It is YOUR patriotic duty to inform yourself!

Chapter 14
Accidental Patriot

Was the Death of the Obama Birth Certificate Verifier Caught on Video?

The pages that follow read like a mystery novel. I believe this was a shrewd scheme by the perpetrators. I appeal to the readers to log on to the website at the end of this document. The information is vital.

Every effort has been extended to seek the author of this important document.

Log on to:

http://accidentialpatriot4.wordpress.com/2014/02/23/see-how-loretta-fuddy-was-murdered-photos-beyond-frightening/

The following excerpts are from the document:

Since the day it was announced that Loretta Fuddy, the Director of the Hawaii Department of Health who verified Obama's birth certificate died mysteriously in a plane crash, there was some question of whether is was really an "accident". The authorities seem to be saying, yes. But, because of her close ties to the fraudulent Obama Birth Certificate, many people fear that she was the most recent in Obama's "dead pool" and haven't stopped looking for real answers. ".

The photos can be found here:

http://butterdezillion.wordpress.com/2014/02/13/extras/ .

The Puentes video originally aired on ABC in January 2014 and can be seen here:

http://abcnews.go.com/US/harrowing-video-hawaiian-plane-crash-inside-cabin/story?id=21484715

Dr. Fuddys death was declared to be from a problem with her heart – natural causes, and we're all supposed to believe that it was all just a tragic accident, but after seeing these photos, all doubt is gone. As I looked through the still shots taken from the video, my blood froze, because I knew what I was seeing. I am seeing a diver do something to Loretta Fuddy, which I assume was murder, and it chills me to the bone. I hope that law enforcement can be made aware of what seems to be shown in these pictures, so they can investigate it. Just look, please. Form your own opinion.

THE PHOTOGRAPHIC EVIDENCE

The series of photos shown below are the actual stills of the events that are shown on Ferdinand Puentes video.

http://abcnews.go.com/US/harrowing-video-hawaiian-plane-crash-inside-cabin/story?id=21484715

These photos have been zoomed and cropped by Butterdezillion. In the GoPro video, the action is actually quite a distance away. You can click on any set to enlarge them to see better.

Loretta Fuddy Murder

So, there you have it. Loretta Fuddy is floating in her life jacket holding hands with her Assistant, Keith Yamamoto. A diver completely dressed in black surfaces momentarily for about 3 seconds and seems to be doing something to her foot or leg.

Greatest Conspiracies

As we know the plane sank within 25 minutes, and it is still visible in the video, there are NOT rescue divers. The two hands holding the foot in picture #5 are what makes me sure of what I'm seeing.

Picture # 5 shows two hands holding the yellow shoe, # 6 shows both hands releasing the shoe.

Even if I'm wrong about the shoe – this IS A DIVER who shouldn't be there and is clearly up to no good. Whatever this is – it is frightening. I hope that the right people are made aware of this and that it can be followed up on appropriately.

FYI -this pictures terrifies me. What kind of world do we live in? The further implication to this photo is that this was a STAGED accident. It is no coincidence that a plane lost its engine within swimming distance of two divers/assassins. We also then have to wonder if the pilot was in on it, unless the divers were ON THE PLANE and the engine was sabotaged. Either way, someone planned this, and Dr. Fuddy is dead.

Blog at Wordpress.com/The Flounder Theme

http://accidentalpatriot4.wordpress.com/tag/loretta-fuddy-accident/

After reading this, and studying it carefully, additional data is warranted (WNH):

1. Where is a map of the location of the airport in relation to the crash site?

2. Was there a crash or a landing? There is a difference.

3. What is the distance in feet, yards or miles from the shoreline to the alleged crash site?

4. What is the estimated depth of sea water at the crash site?

5. Did the airplane have a compartment large enough to hide two fully dressed divers with gear? Could they evacuate the plane after the plane crash without being seen?

6. How many people were listed on the plane's manifest? What were their names?

7. Who organized the plane trip? What was the destination? What was the purpose of the trip?

8. Did the plane engines have a malfunction at take off? Were there witnesses to any unusual engine sounds?

9. How many minutes was the plane in the air before it crashed?

10. Did the pilots issue a crash warning?

11. Did anyone hear the conversations between the crew of the plane?

12. After the plane crashed, were all of the passengers accounted for with no injuries reported?

13. Was there a small boat near the crash site?

14. Was there a floating marker anchored near the crash site?

15. Approximately how many minutes did it take for the pilots to vacate the plane?

16. How many minutes did it take for the divers to appear after everyone was safely in the water?

17. Where were the pilots?

18. Why were there two divers who suddenly appeared like sharks at the crash site, grabbing Dr. Fuddy's shoe and foot, Dr. Fuddy struggling to free herself from the diver? This caused the diver to lose his grip when she jerked her leg to the surface. Within a few seconds after this struggle, Dr. Fuddy was dead.

19. Is it possible, as the data indicates, that a surveillance team was assigned to Dr. Loretta Fuddy to relay data to the perpetrators for easy identification from below the surface of the water? The data indicates the divers were waiting below the surface for the crash to occur.

20. Who was the owner of the plane?

21. Was the plane salvaged to determine the cause of the crash?

22. Has anyone obtained the service records of the plane?

23. Who were the pilots of the plane?

Many unanswered questions remain!

Chapter 15
Our Morals and Religion are Seriously Threatened

President Obama is pressing for gay marriage across the United States of America. Again, Obama is campaigning for Democratic votes.

When the earth was formed and all living species were active, what happened to each of the species? Humans ended up at the top of the food chain. Other species kept to themselves as separate groups. Who has seen a lion mating with a grizzly bear? A crow mating with a blue bird? Where is there evidence that a rockfish mates with a trout?

The ComSocs brainwashed Congress and the public over the years to change the true meaning of the separation of church and state as it was intended. Now the ComSocs have won another battle concerning gay rights when a male can marry another male and a female can marry another female.

When a male mates with another male and gives birth to a child, case solved. When a female mates with another female without mating with a male and gives birth to a child, case solved.

Look it up in the <u>Merriam-Webster Dictionary</u>. The word *Marry* is defined as: *1) to join as husband and wife according to law or custom; 2) To take as husband or wife; wed; 3) To enter into a close union – married.* The husband is a male. The wife is a female.

Over generations and for all time, a marriage was between a male and a female (Man and Woman). The brainwashing has been successful by the ComSocs. Our laws, our customs, our religious beliefs, our freedom has been the battleground of the ComSocs.

To repeat: The people of the United States must wake up to reality. The main tools of the ComSocs were and still are the minorities, the uninformed, the voters who still think they are voting for the Democratic Party. They have been brainwashed.

Where are all the religious denominational headquarter leaders? Where are all the denominational preachers – no matter what the title? What happened to denominational creeds and beliefs? Has religion disappeared and the churches have become social clubs? All are in disrespect to the God of the universe.

The obvious problem is fighting the ACLU with their large grants of taxpayer money and large donations from organizations and billionaires, which is a disadvantage. However, it is not a deterrent for all denominations.

Our moral structure is being destroyed. All you need to do is to take time for a recap. Be honest with yourself. What are you hearing and viewing on the television? Curse words; filthy words; sex products; sexual actions; and crime. If, by chance, you see some good news or programming for our ears and eyes, and for those of our children and grandchildren – well, that is a miracle!

The advertisement of a sex pill, discussing an erection that may last four hours, filthy talk at mealtime on the evening news with children present. If a person cannot buy the product without a prescription, then why broadcast it for everyone to hear! The manufacturers and news networks are blatant and disingenuous to our children and parents. Yes, I realize it is legal. The donations and big tax breaks for expenditures drives this type of illicit advertising. Just my opinion.

Back in the 1930s and 1940s, we had prayer and scripture reading in the public schools. There was never a protest or lawsuit to eliminate prayer or scripture reading in our school system. Why our Constitution was legal years ago, but our Constitution is considered illegal in 2014 according to the ComSocs?

Our country was founded on religious beliefs and anyone who does not like the United States Constitution is free to leave.

Not all is lost! We must vote the ComSocs out of the Federal Government in the election in 2016.

Chapter 16
Climate

Some Interesting Observations

1. The winter of 2014 in the Chesapeake Bay produced such cold temperatures that it killed many blue crabs.

2. The volcano that erupted(in Chile in approximately 2010) did so with such great force that it cause the earth to tilt 3° off of its normal axis as reported by a scientist from the news media.

3. "North" seems to be moving – (San Francisco) – The Associated Press (Excerpt from article) Earth's north magnetic pole is drifting away from North America and toward Siberia at such a clip that Alaska might lose its spectacular Northern Lights in the next 50 years, reported by a scientist from an American Geophysical Union Meeting. The earth magnetic shield has decreased 10% over the past 150 years.

4. The winter of 2014 produced a freeze at the Great Lakes. It was reported the ice in the lakes was thicker than any previous recordings. In the area of North Dakota, it was reported the depth of total snow on the ground was greater than any depth in recorded history. From the news media.

5. Global Warming stopped 16 years ago, based on data through August 2012 – The Richmond Times Dispatch

6. The moon is drifting away from the earth at the rate of ½ inch per year – from a news media science article.

7. The sun's flares are larger and extend farther into space, reaching closer to earth. From the news media.

8. The earth, over millions of years, has tilted north to south three times, maintaining its orbit. The earth has had 5 ice ages – The Richmond Times Dispatch

9. Several years ago, scientists were drilling into glaciers at the North Pole. When they removed the ice cores, they discovered dinosaur bones and plants (ferns) which proves the earth shifts on its orbit, causing climate change which is a natural phenomenon that occurs over the course of time.

Global Warming – Facts are Facts and We've Been Had!

1. Fairfax – by Walter Williams (Creators Syndicate) from The Richmond Times Dispatch. My scanning through the article revealed (as I interpreted it) that some scientists were skeptical. They were called traitors (indicating to me the conspiracies never end). The article stated lies were told and academic fraud was engaged. The belief and faked data passed on to journalists.

    Editors of professional journals who disagreed with the group that global warming is caused by human beings were forced to resign from their jobs.

    Science data from the Medieval Warm Period (MWP) from 800 AD to 1300AD indicates the earth was much warmer that it is now.

    Who are these people, the environmental extremists who have the power to force resignations of people who do not agree with their theory? Other articles contained data about the extremist's actions to coerce nations around the world to provide multi-millions of dollars to their group.

2. In Anchorage Alaska, the recent winter had snow falls over 94 inches up to January 2014. This is more than the 68 inches it normally accumulates – The Associated Press, Richmond Time Dispatch

3. Consider these inconvenient realities about planetary warming. The National Aeronautics and Space Administration

(NASA) reported the ice caps on planet Mars near the South Pole region are melting – Ross Mackenzie, The Richmond Times Dispatch

4. The Sun: On the same day Al Gore (who does not know beans from a bull's foot) was blowing his horn in a speech to Congress, NASA announced solar activity is rendering the sun hotter than previously believed. The Danish Meteorological Institute stated there is a direct correlation between solar flare-ups (sunspots) and rising temperatures on earth.

5. Groundskeepers Up Against Time: Rough 2014 Winter has Left Ballparks in North Frozen Solid – by The Associated Press, from The Richmond Times Dispatch

6. Carbon Offsets – New Penance Offers Absolution to Environmental Hypocrites – Victor Davis Hanson for The Richmond Times Dispatch

7. In an October, 2007 article by the Bloomsberg News Service entitled *UN Study a Bleak Forecast for Planet* stated the world's economy was at risk unless warming and other issues were fixed.

> Excerpts from the article: The United Nations report prepared by about 390 scientists worldwide and reviewed by 1000 others points to an urgent need for political leadership on climate change. China and India are exempt from making cuts under the Kyoto Protocol treaty. [**Very Interesting. WNH**]

Concluding Thoughts About the Climate

The rotation of planets, the sun flares, the drifting moon effecting the tidal cycles of the oceans, low to high (for example: the tide fluctuates on the coast of South Korea (thirty feet opposite China) all are responsible for global warming. As the moon drifts farther away from earth, the tidal cycles change, causing the sea levels to remain higher at low time. The tilting of the earth, the magnetic North Pole drifting toward Siberia, the earth's 3° tilt off of its normal axis are responsible for some parts of the earth have had record high and low temperatures. The earth's crust is being weakened. Another story.

If the citizens of the United States believe the brainwashing rhetoric, then this is what will happen: **Vote for Me – I Am Solving Global Warming.** Vote for them and this is what will happen: the government will be empowered to have more control of the people. We will be required to pay additional taxes. More money will flow to the soothsayers. The end result? No climate problems solved!

Everything is aimed at the United States. The ComSocs blame the USA for the world's problems. All nations are creating the problem. However, no one person, no group, no one nation have the ability or the power to alter, change, fix the impact on planet Earth from the Moon, the Sun, the normal cycle of the Earth or from space.

Yes, there are things we can do. Stop cutting down all out trees. Invent a product that performs like tree lumber to save our depleting oxygen level – the key element for survival on Earth.

About the Authors

2014 – Norman is a "young" 91-year-old World War II Veteran. He was a Navy Corpsman who served in the Marine Corps in the pacific theatre. He attended an architectural university after the war and was employed by an architect with great experience.

Over the years, Norman accumulated additional architectural and engineering experience.

Norman acquired a position with a USA corporation, performing corporate duties. He was awarded two national awards at Construction Specification Institute (a professional organization) conventions. Later, Norman became a professional member.

A State Commissioner of the Department of Mental Hygiene and Hospitals announced the appointment of Norman as Assistant Director of Capital Outlays.

His desire to keep moving on up gave him the motivation to organize his own business. In the corporate structure, his services provided consulting, design, sales and construction. Norman received two additional national awards. He retired at 66.

Kristy St Pere – Norman's daughter – was interested in the medical profession from the age of 16 years. Kristy would visit the local rescue squad organization at their previous place of residence. Later Kristy received training as a paramedic. She has continued her medical training through the years. She currently serves as a Division Captain, in public service with a city fire department.

Index

Greatest Conspiracies

www.ingramcontent.com/pod-product-compliance
Lightning Source LLC
Chambersburg PA
CBHW060204290526
45789CB00003B/1150